MATH FUN FOR
MINECRAFTERS

Grades 1-2

Illustrated by Amanda Brack

Sky Pony Press
New York

Sky Pony Press books may be purchased in bulk at special discounts for sales promotion, corporate gifts, fund-raising, or educational purposes. Special editions can also be created to specifications. For details, contact the Special Sales Department, Sky Pony Press, 307 West 36th Street, 11th Floor, New York, NY 10018 or info@skyhorsepublishing.com.

Sky Pony® is a registered trademark of Skyhorse Publishing, Inc.®, a Delaware corporation.

Minecraft® is a registered trademark of Notch Development AB.
The Minecraft game is copyright © Mojang AB.

Visit our website at www.skyponypress.com.

10 9 8 7 6 5 4

Library of Congress Cataloging-in-Publication Data is available on file.

Cover design by Brian Peterson
Cover illustration by Bill Greenhead
Interior art by Amanda Brack
Book design by Kevin Baier

Print ISBN: 978-1-5107-3760-0

Printed in China

A NOTE TO PARENTS

When you want to reinforce classroom skills at home, it's crucial to have kid-friendly learning materials. This *Math Fun for Minecrafters* workbook transforms math practice into an irresistible adventure complete with diamond swords, zombies, skeletons, and creepers. That means less arguing over homework and more fun overall.

Math Fun for Minecrafters is also fully aligned with National Common Core Standards for 1st and 2nd grade math. What does that mean, exactly? All of the problems in this book correspond to what your child is expected to learn in school. This eliminates confusion and builds confidence for greater homework-time success!

As an added benefit to parents, the pages of this workbook are color coded to help you target specific skill areas as needed. Each color represents one of the four categories of Common Core math instruction. Use the chart below to guide you in understanding the different skills being taught at your child's school and to pinpoint areas where they may need extra practice.

BLUE	Operations and Algebraic Thinking
PINK	**Numbers and Operations in Base 10**
GREEN	Measurement and Data
ORANGE	Geometry

As the workbook progresses, the math problems become more advanced. Encourage your child to progress at his or her own pace. Learning is best when students are challenged, but not frustrated. What's most important is that your Minecrafter is engaged in his or her own learning.

Whether it's the joy of seeing their favorite game characters on every page or the thrill of solving challenging problems just like Steve and Alex, there is something in this workbook to entice even the most reluctant math student.

Happy adventuring!

ADDITION BY GROUPING

Circle groups of 10. Then count and write the numbers.

Example:

1. 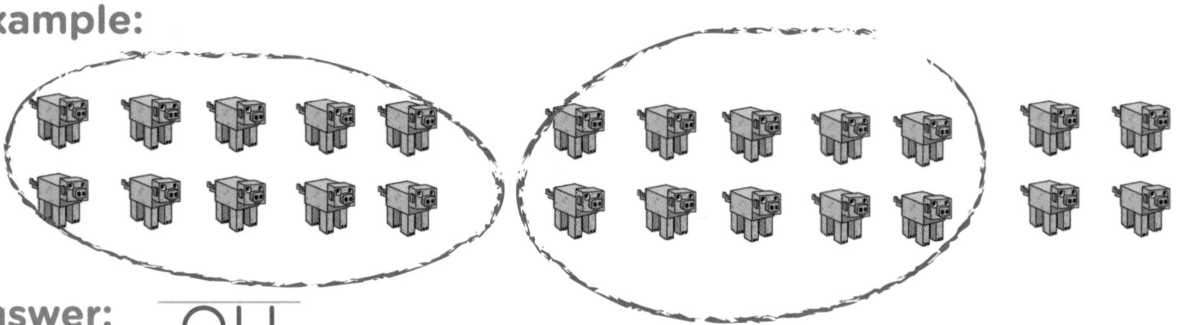

Answer: 24

2. 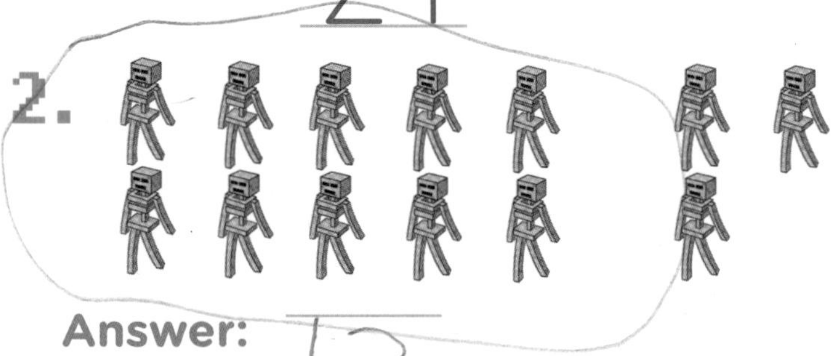

Answer: 13

3. 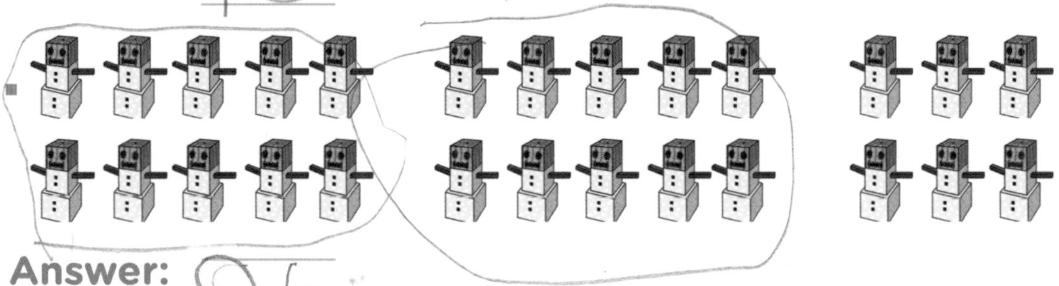

Answer: 26

4. 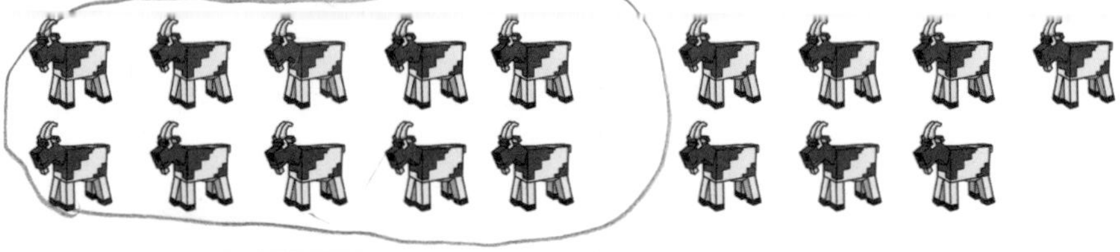

Answer: 12

5. 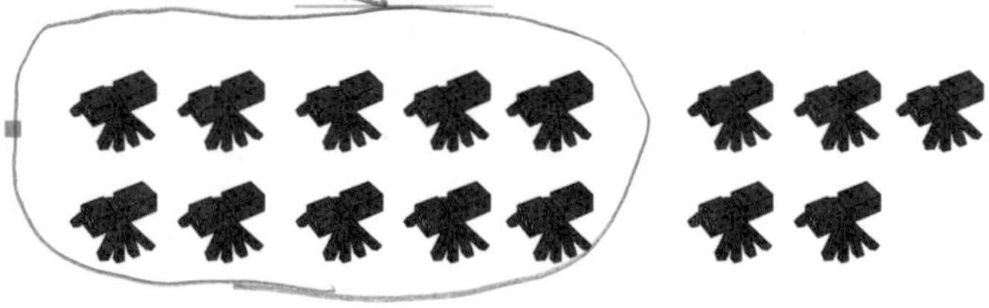

Answer: 15

MYSTERY MESSAGE
WITH ADDITION AND SUBTRACTION

Add or subtract. Then use the letters to fill in the blanks below and reveal the answer to Steve's joke.

1. 4 + 8 = **12** F

2. 9 − 3 = **6** C

3. 6 + 8 = **14** O

4. 8 + 3 = **11** A

5. 8 − 1 = **7** K

6. 9 + 7 = **16** B

7. 8 − 3 = **5** L

8. 4 + 9 = **13** E

Q: What's the top social network for Minecrafters?

A: FAcE _____ BLOcK

COPY THE LETTERS FROM THE ANSWERS ABOVE TO SOLVE THE MYSTERY.

F A c E
12 11 6 13

B L O c K
16 5 14 6 7

5

ZOMBIE'S GUIDE TO PLACE VALUE

Use the number on each zombie to fill in the place-value chart. Then, write the number in tally marks.

Example:

1.

Tens	Ones
2	4

HHT HHT HHT HHT   IIII

2.

Tens	Ones
3	7

3.

Tens	Ones
4	1

4.

Tens	Ones
7	2

5.

Tens	Ones
6	3

6.

Tens	Ones
5	0

7.

Tens	Ones
9	8

SKIP COUNT CHALLENGE

Count by 2s and fill in the empty spaces to keep Steve at a safe distance from the blaze.

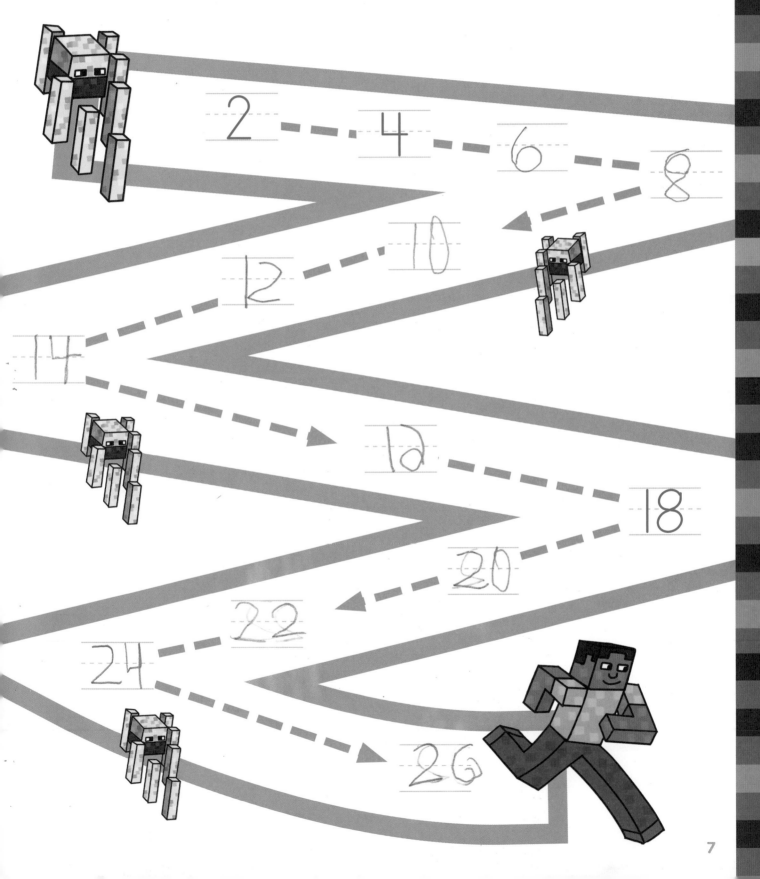

TELLING TIME

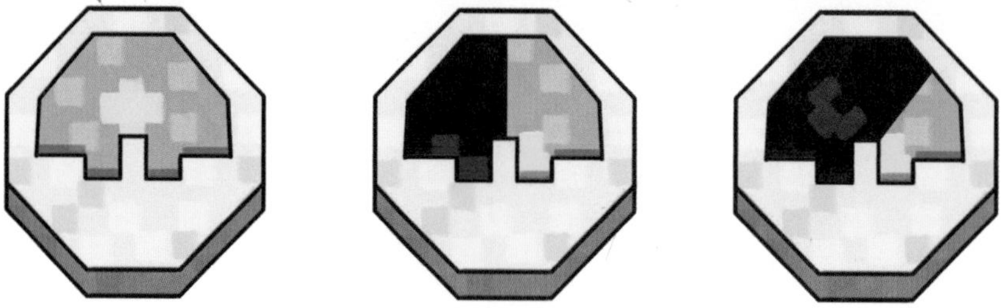

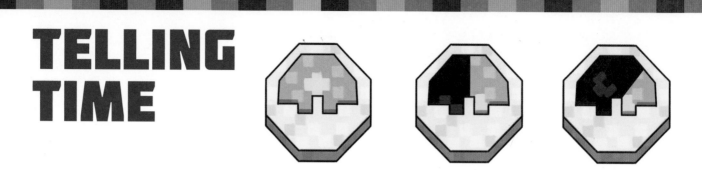

Look at the clocks below and write the time in the space provided:

Example:

1.

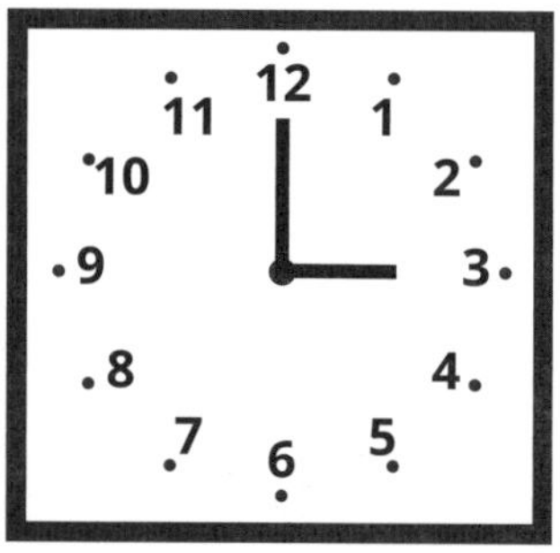

Answer: 3:00

2.

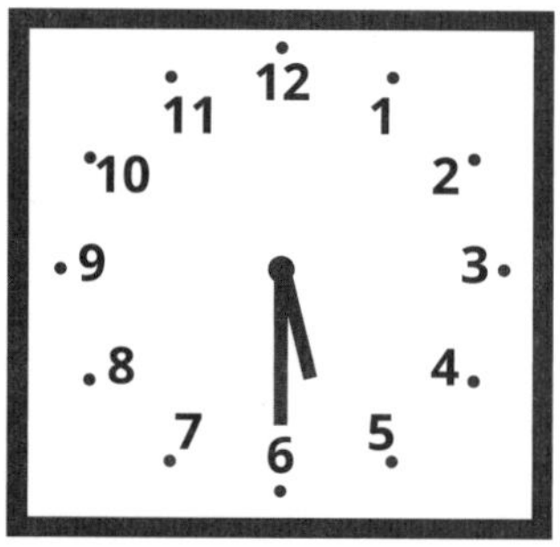

Answer: 5:30

3.

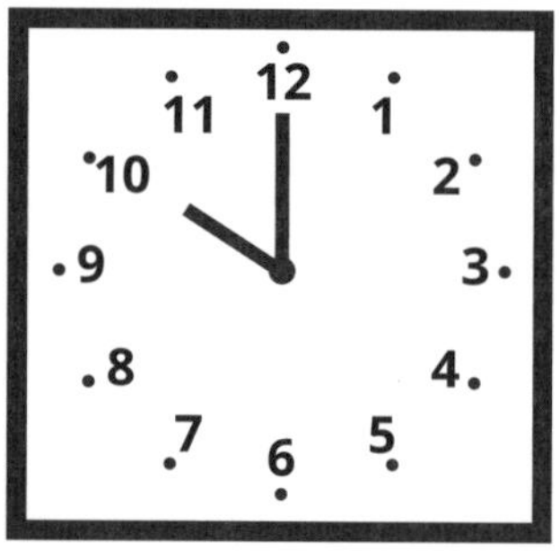

Answer: 11:00

4.

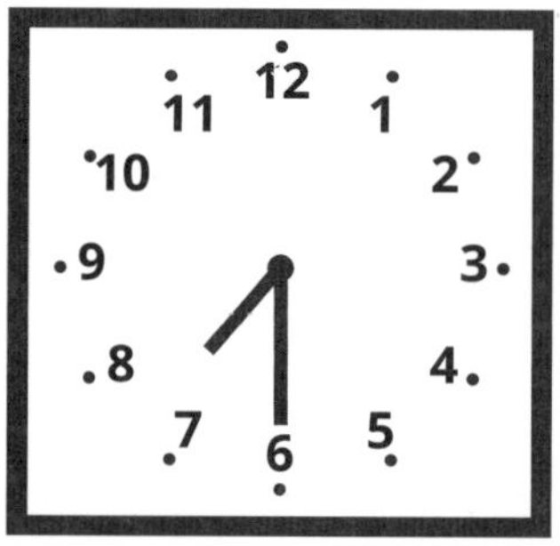

Answer: 7:30

5.

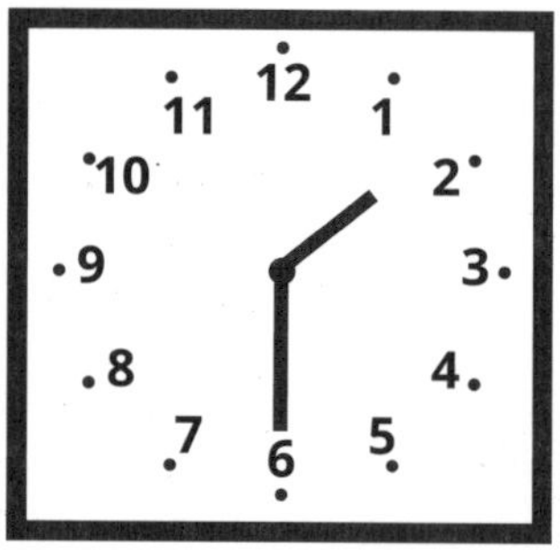

Answer: 1:30

6.

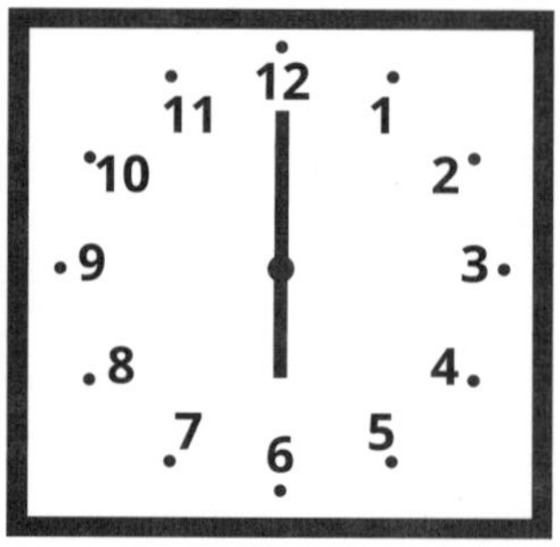

Answer: 6:00

COUNTING MONEY

The villagers are letting you trade coins for emeralds.
Add up your coins to see how much money you have.

25¢   10¢   5¢   1¢

1. 25¢ + 10¢ + 5¢ + 5¢ = 45 ¢

2. 10¢ + 5¢ + 5¢ + 1¢ =

3. 25¢ + 5¢ + 1¢ =

4. 25¢ + 10¢ + 5¢ + 1¢ =

5. 10¢ + 10¢ + 5¢ + 5¢ + 1¢ =

6. 25¢ + 5¢ + 5¢ + 5¢ + 1¢ =

7. 25¢ + 10¢ + 10¢ + 1¢ + 1¢ =

HARDCORE MODE: *Try this hardcore math challenge!*

8. One villager charges 30¢ for each emerald. How many dimes do you need in order to buy an emerald?

Answer:

ADVENTURES IN GEOMETRY

Let's learn about fractions! Count the number of squares in the crafting grid below, and write it on the line.

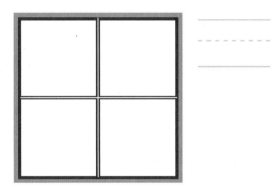

1. Color three of the four squares green

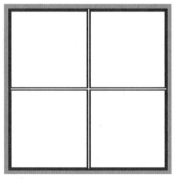

This is called three-fourths, or ¾.

2. Steve breaks this crafting grid into two equal parts. Color one of the two parts yellow.

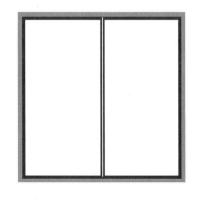

This is called one half, or ½.

3. Count the rectangles in the experience bar below. Write the number here: _____

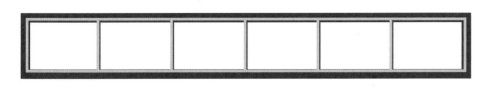

4. This experience bar is divided into 3 equal parts. Color one part blue.

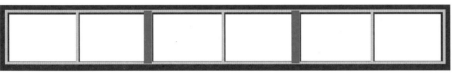

This is called one third, or ⅓.

5. This experience bar is divided into 3 equal parts. Color two parts blue.

This is called two thirds, or ⅔.

HARDCORE MODE: *Try this hardcore math challenge!*
This health bar shows 9 hearts. Color in 3 hearts below.

♡ ♡ ♡ ♡ ♡ ♡ ♡ ♡ ♡

Circle the fraction that describes how many are colored in:

    A. 1/2   **B.** 1/4   **C.** 1/3

WORD PROBLEMS

Read the problem carefully. Use the picture to help you solve the problem. Fill in your answer.

Example:

You get 8 minutes of daylight in Minecraft. You lose 4 minutes building a shelter and finding food. How many minutes are left?

8 – 4 = 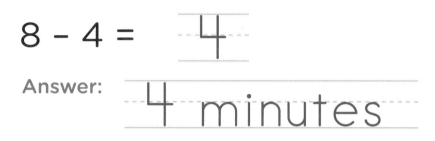 4

Answer: 4 minutes

1. You need 4 wooden planks to make a crafting table, but you only have 2. How many more planks do you need?

   Answer: 4 – 2 = 2 planks

2. There are 7 empty spaces in your inventory bar. You fill 3 spaces with tools. How many empty spaces do you have?

   Answer: 4

3. You shear a mooshroom cow and 7 red mushrooms appear. You eat 4 of them. How many mushrooms are left?

   Answer: 3

4. You have 5 goats on your farm. You add 3 cows to the farm. How many animals do you have?

Answer: 8

5. You have 6 glass blocks. You get 3 more blocks. How many glass blocks do you have?

Answer: 9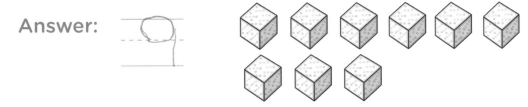

6. There are 7 zombies chasing you. Thankfully, 4 of them fall in a lava pit! How many zombies are still chasing you?

Answer: 3

7. Alex has 5 axes in her inventory. She crafts 2 more axes. How many axes does she have?

Answer: 7

8. Yesterday 3 skeletons spawned in the Overworld. Today 6 spawned. How many more skeletons spawned today than yesterday?

Answer: 3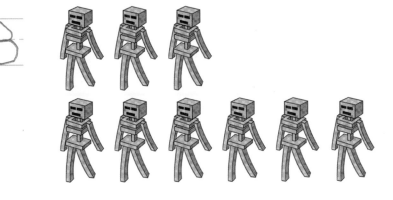

CREEPER'S GUIDE TO PLACE VALUE

Read the number above each creeper to fill in the place-value chart. Then, write the number in tally marks.

Example:

1.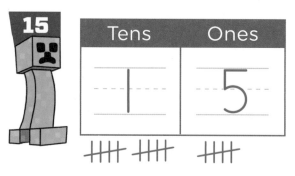

Tens	Ones
1	5

IIII IIII   IIII

2. **27**

Tens	Ones

3. **86**

Tens	Ones

4. **32**

Tens	Ones

5. **71**

Tens	Ones

6. **60**

Tens	Ones

7. **54**

Tens	Ones

SKIP COUNT CHALLENGE

The baby zombie is tired after a long night of fighting. Count by 3s and help him find shelter before the sun rises.

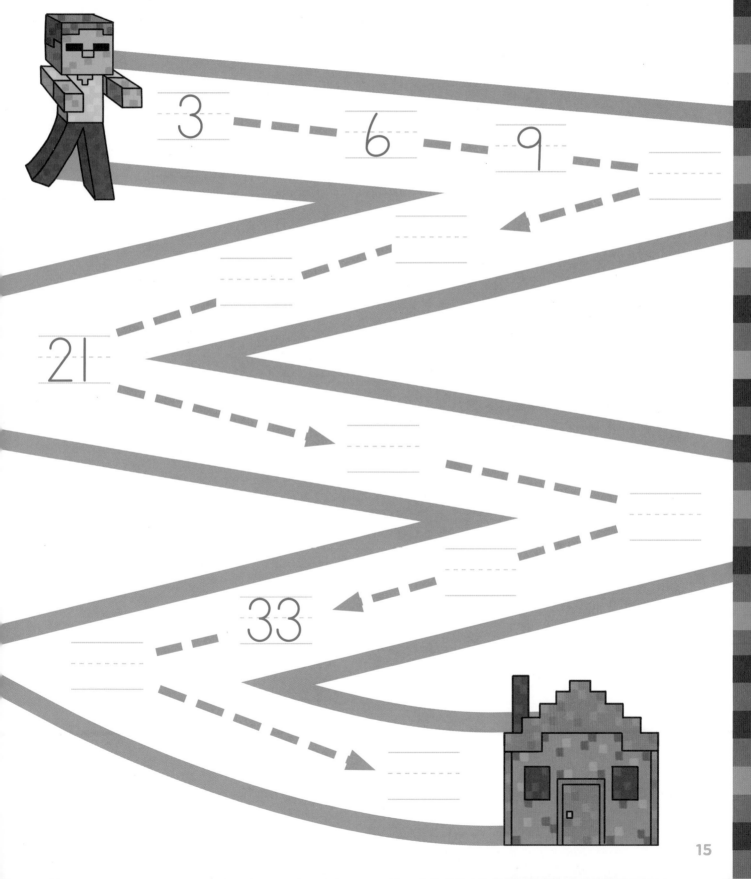

3   6   9

21

33

ALL IN A DAY'S WORK

A Minecrafter's first day is very busy!
Match the time for each task on the left with a clock on the right.

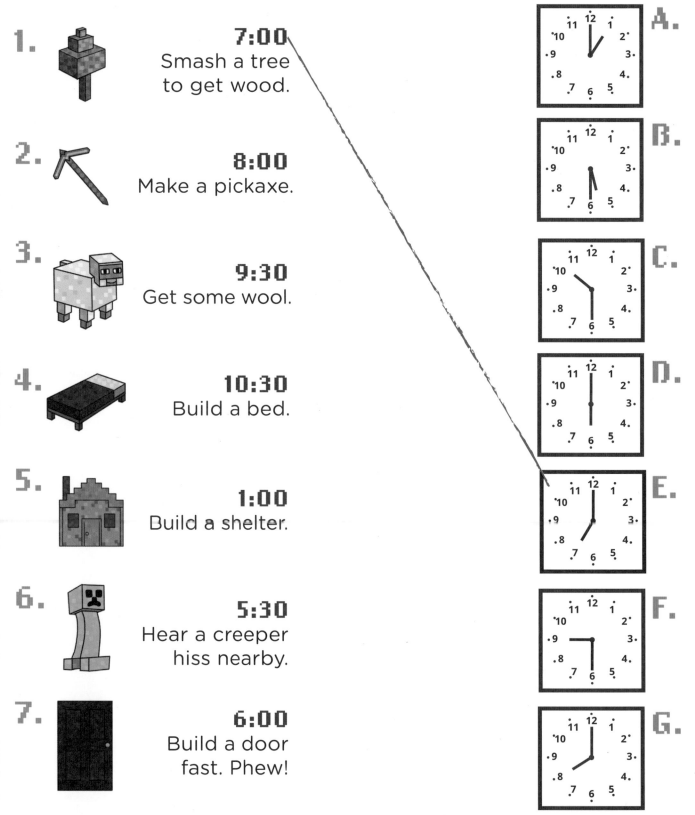

1. **7:00**
Smash a tree
to get wood.

2. **8:00**
Make a pickaxe.

3. **9:30**
Get some wool.

4. **10:30**
Build a bed.

5. **1:00**
Build a shelter.

6. **5:30**
Hear a creeper
hiss nearby.

7. **6:00**
Build a door
fast. Phew!

A.

B.

C.

D.

E.

F.

G.

TIME FOR CLOCKS

Draw a big hand and a little hand on the clock to show the time.

Example:

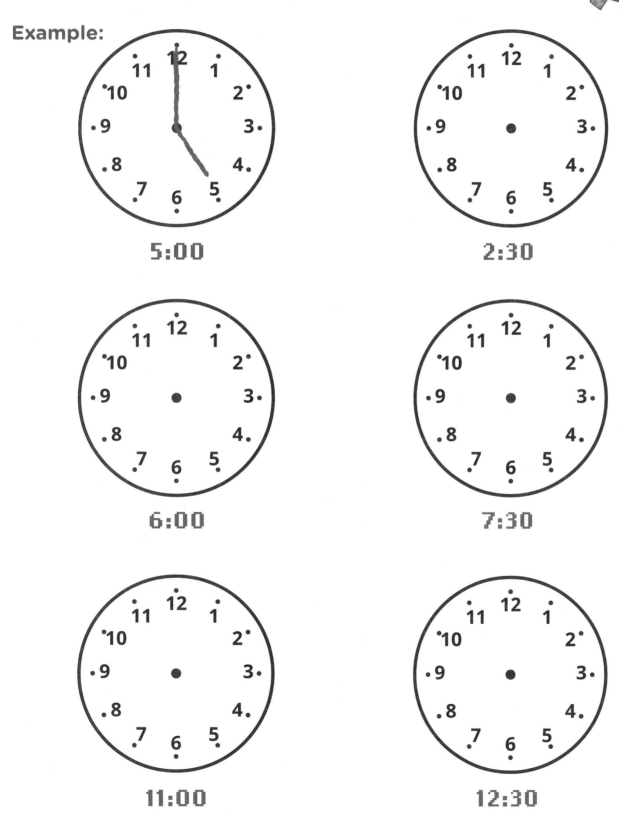

5:00

2:30

6:00

7:30

11:00

12:30

LEARNING ABOUT SHAPES

Draw along the dotted line to complete each shape. Connect the name of the shape to the correct drawing.

1. triangle

2. trapezoid

3. square

4. rectangle

A.

B.

C.

D.

FIND THE SHAPES

Look at the items below and and use the word box to write the name:

square	circle	rectangle

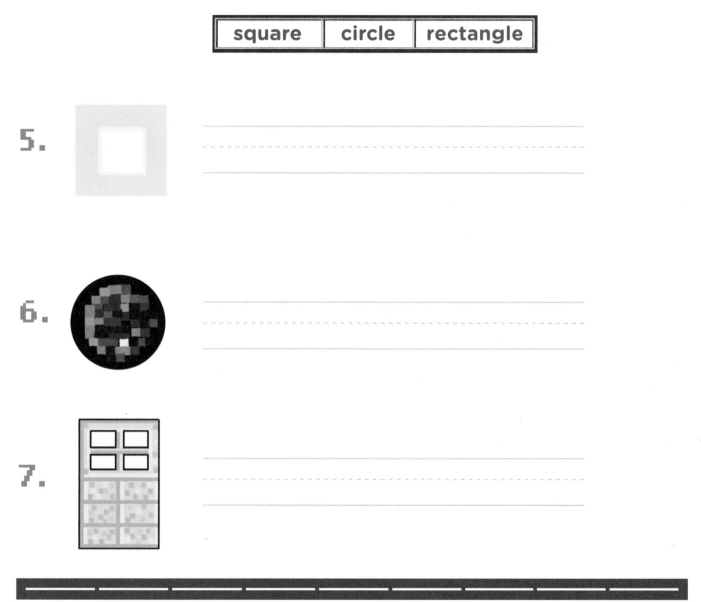

5. _____

6. _____

7. _____

---

8. HARDCORE MODE: *Try this hardcore math challenge!*
Find 7 triangles in this pile of diamonds and circle them.

ADDITION BY GROUPING

Circle groups of 10 weapons and tools. Then count and write the total number.

Example:

1.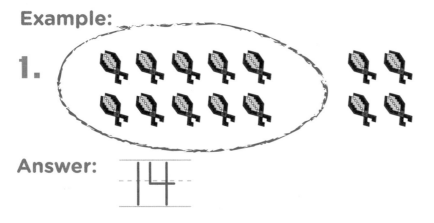

Answer: 14

2.

Answer: _____

3.

Answer: _____

4.

Answer: _____

MYSTERY MESSAGE
WITH ADDITION AND SUBTRACTION

Add or subtract. Then use the letters to fill in the blanks below and reveal the answer to Steve's joke.

1. $12 + 8 =$ 20 B

2. $11 - 8 =$ _____ A

3. $19 - 3 =$ _____ L

4. $14 + 3 =$ _____ Y

5. $11 + 2 =$ _____ K

6. $18 - 7 =$ _____ T

7. $12 - 3 =$ _____ P

8. $13 - 5 =$ _____ R

9. $17 - 5 =$ _____ O

10. $15 - 9 =$ _____ C

Q: What kind of party do Minecrafters throw?

COPY THE LETTERS FROM THE ANSWERS ABOVE TO FIND OUT.

B _____ _____ _____ _____
20   16   12   6   13

_____ _____ _____ _____ _____
9   3   8   11   17

THE ENDER DRAGON NUMBER CHALLENGE

Match the Ender Dragon with the description of the number.

1.

Tens	Ones
7	6

2.

Tens	Ones
1	7

3.

Tens	Ones
6	4

4.

Tens	Ones
3	1

5.

Tens	Ones
9	8

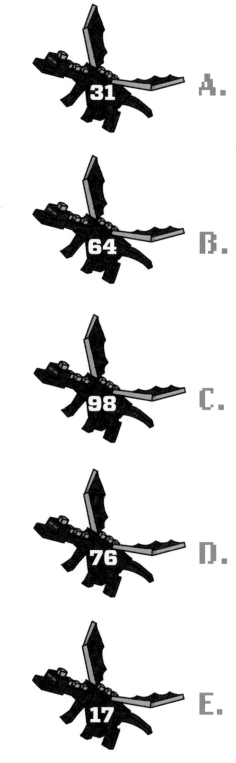

A. 31

B. 64

C. 98

D. 76

E. 17

SKIP COUNT CHALLENGE

Count by 5s to help tame the ocelot. Feed it enough fish on this numbered path and you'll have a new pet!

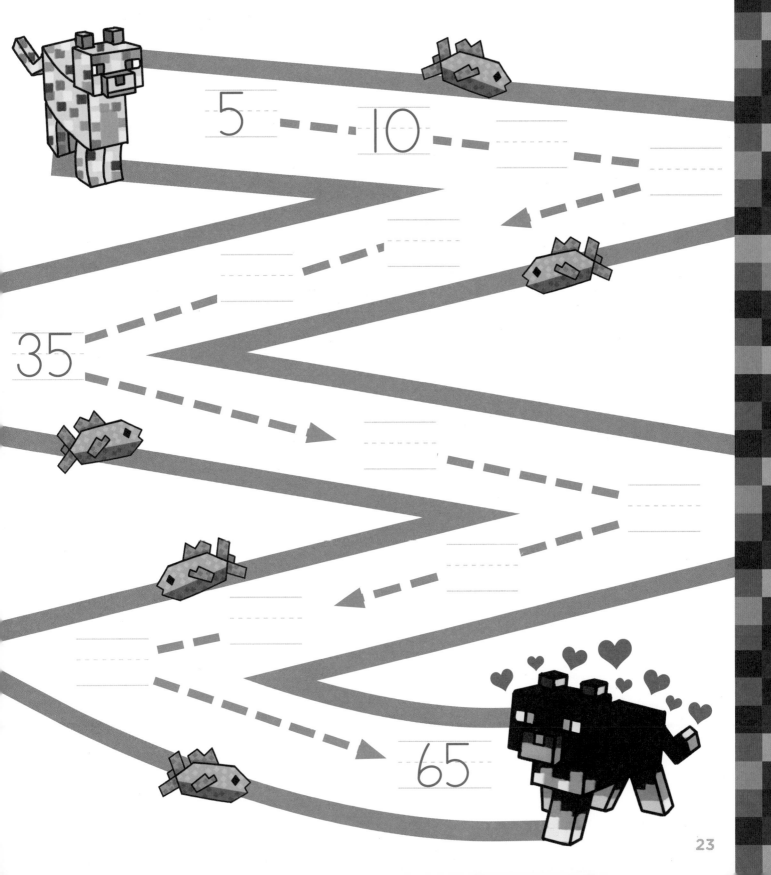

5 — 10 — _____

_____

35

_____

65

COMPARING RAIL TRACKS

Alex built 3 rail tracks. Compare the number of ties on each track and write your answers below.

How many ties (boards going from side to side) are on each track?

A.

B.

C.

1. Which track has the most ties?

2. Which track has the fewest ties?

3. How many more ties does track A have compared to track C?

_____ **ties.**

4. Draw your own rail track, called rail track D, in the space below. It must have more ties than rail track C, but less than rail track A. Color it in and add a rail cart full of loot!

D.

5. How many ties does your track have? _____

6. Fill in the rest of this table to keep track of all the different tracks.

Track	Number of Ties
A	6
B	
C	
D	

ADVENTURES IN GEOMETRY

Trace the dotted line to divide these shapes into 2 equal parts. Then color one half (½) of the shape.

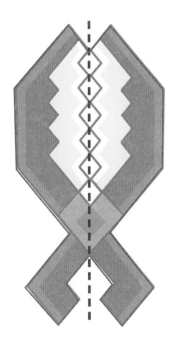

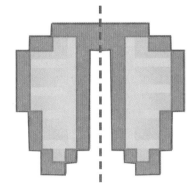

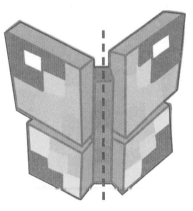

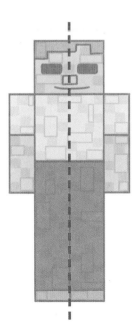

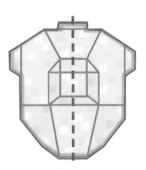

Trace the dotted line to divide these shapes into 4 equal parts. Then color in one fourth (¼) of each shape below.

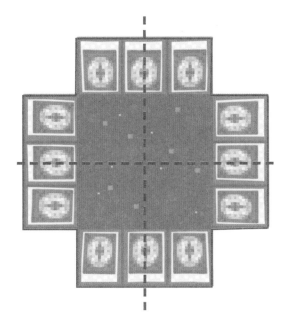

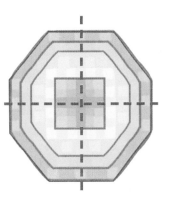

Color in one third of this wooden plank:

⅓

Color in three fourths of this wooden plank:

¾

WORD PROBLEMS

Read the problem carefully. Look at the picture and fill in your answer.

Example:

1. Alex eats 2 carrots. She attacks zombies, and they drop 3 more carrots and 2 potatoes for her to eat. How many food items does she eat all together?

$$2+3+2=7$$

Answer: 7

2. Steve collects 5 hay bales to build a stable, 2 hay bales to build a barn, and 3 more hay bales to feed his horses. How many hay bales does he have in all?

Answer:

3. Steve sees 15 zombies on his adventures. He destroys 5 with a trap and 6 more with his sword. How many zombies are left?

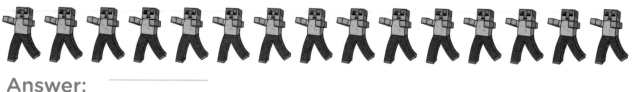

Answer:

4. In one day, Alex makes 7 swords, 3 bows and arrows, and 8 shovels to attack mobs. How many weapons did she make in all?

Answer:

5. Alex gets 4 cookies from trading with a villager. She gets 6 more cookies later in the day and 2 more cookies in the morning. How many cookies does she have in all?

Answer: _____

6. You start your game with 18 hunger points. You lose 3 points running away from a creeper. You lose 5 more points attacking skeletons. How many hunger points are left?

Answer: _____

7. You start your game with 8 items in your inventory. You remove 3 tools and 2 food items. How many items are left in your inventory?

Answer: _____

8. Steve loves his pet cats. He has 3 in a fenced area outside, 5 in his house, and 4 in another fenced area. How many pet cats does he have?

Answer: _____

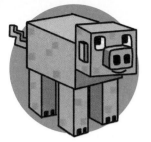

PIG'S GUIDE TO PLACE VALUE

Use the number below each pig to fill in the place value chart.

Example:

1.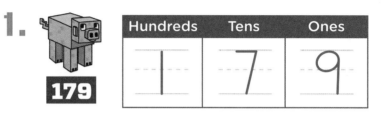

179

Hundreds	Tens	Ones
1	7	9

2. 235

Hundreds	Tens	Ones

3. 467

Hundreds	Tens	Ones

4. 596

Hundreds	Tens	Ones

5. 708

Hundreds	Tens	Ones

6. 430

Hundreds	Tens	Ones

7. 264

Hundreds	Tens	Ones

SKIP COUNT CHALLENGE

Fill in the blank spaces as you count from 110 to 125 and help the horse find her way back to the barn.

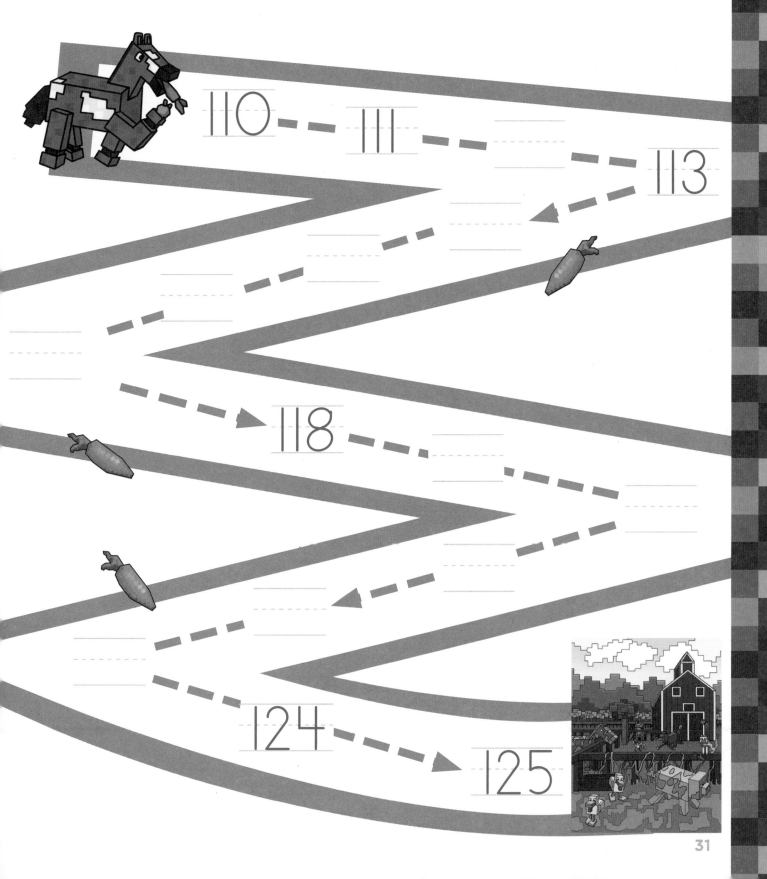

110 --- 111 --- 113

118

124 --- 125

MOBS AND MONSTERS

Video game characters are sometimes called mobs. Add an X to the boxes that describe each mob in the table below. Then answer the questions.

	Skeleton	Ghast	Cave Spider	Snow Golem
0 Legs				
2 Legs				
More than 2 Legs				

1. How many mobs have more than 2 legs?

2. How many mobs have 2 legs or fewer?

3. Which 2 mobs have no arms?

COUNTING MONEY

Steve wants to feed his farm animals the following items. Find out how much money each item costs and write the amount in the space provided.

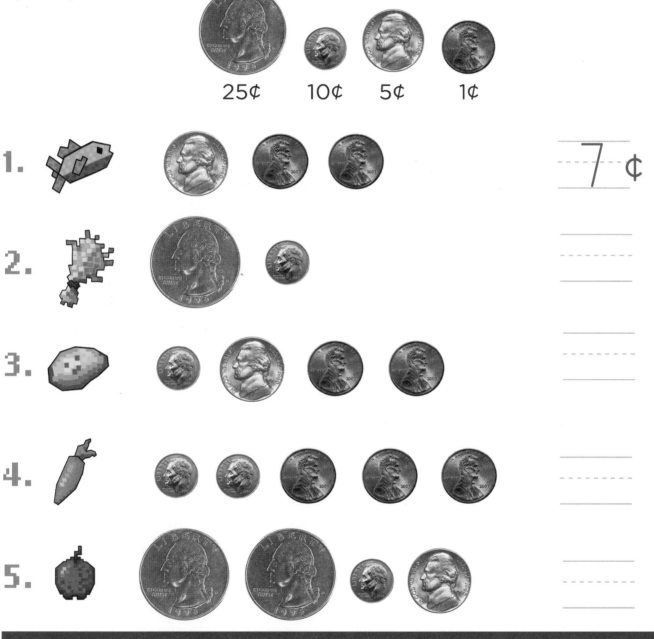

25¢   10¢   5¢   1¢

1.   ___7___ ¢

2.   _____

3.   _____

4.   _____

5.   _____

HARDCORE MODE: *Try this hardcore math challenge!*

6. How much money does Steve need to buy 2 fish and 3 carrots? Add them up to find out!

Answer: _____

ADVENTURES IN GEOMETRY: SPOT THE SHAPES

Look at the diamond chestplate and answer the questions.
Use the shapes below to help you.

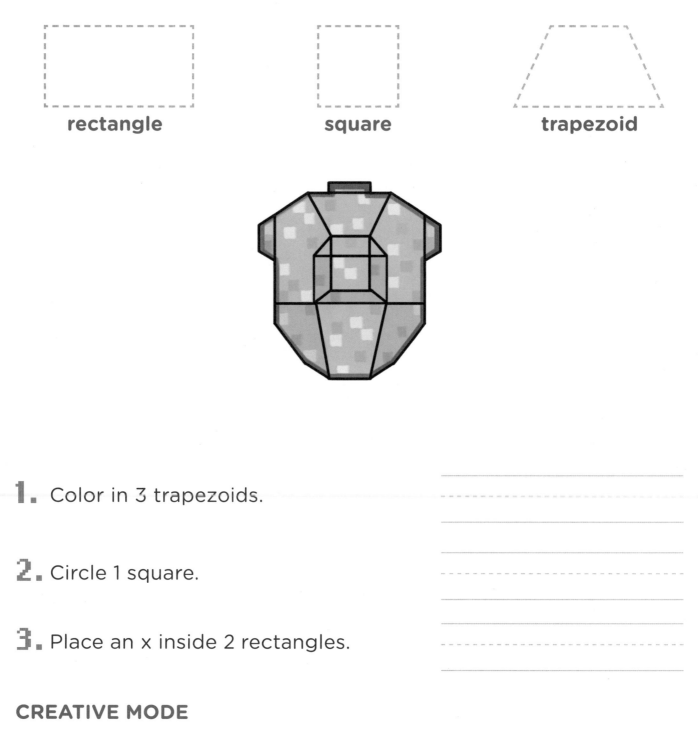

rectangle   square   trapezoid

1. Color in 3 trapezoids.

2. Circle 1 square.

3. Place an x inside 2 rectangles.

CREATIVE MODE

Use a pencil or pen to change the square into 2 triangles!

Draw Alex wearing a chestplate like this one. Use as many shapes as you can. Add fun details and color!

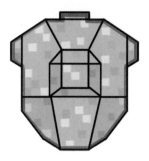

MUSHROOM ADDITION

Add the ones and then the tens to get the answer.

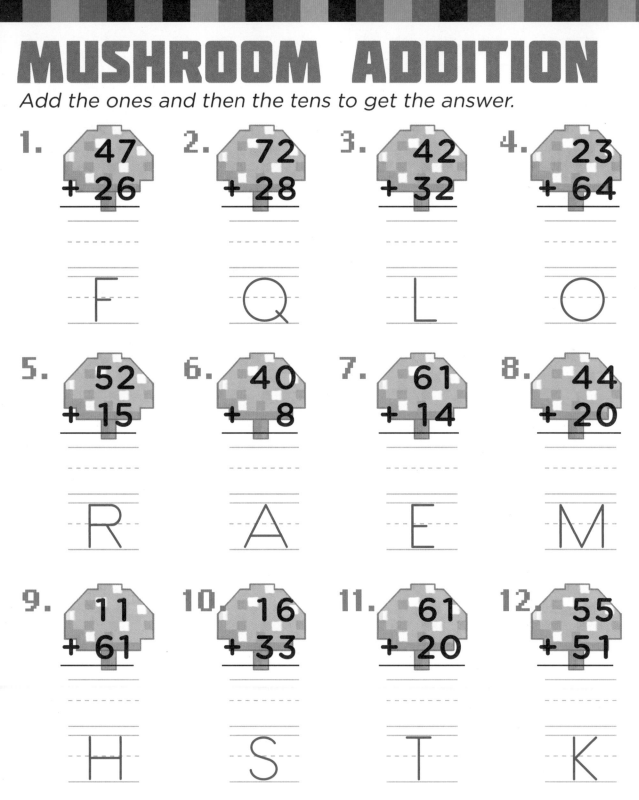

1. 47
  + 26
  _____

  F

2. 72
  + 28
  _____

  Q

3. 42
  + 32
  _____

  L

4. 23
  + 64
  _____

  O

5. 52
  + 15
  _____

  R

6. 40
  + 8
  _____

  A

7. 61
  + 14
  _____

  E

8. 44
  + 20
  _____

  M

9. 11
  + 61
  _____

  H

10. 16
  + 33
  _____

  S

11. 61
  + 20
  _____

  T

12. 55
  + 51
  _____

  K

HIDDEN MESSAGE:

Odd numbers end in 1, 3, 5, 7, or 9. Circle the ODD numbered answers above. Write the letter from those blocks in order from left to right below to spell out the name of a biome with lots of mushrooms:

_____ _____ _____ _____ _____ _____

_____ _____ _____ _____ _____ _____

SUBTRACTION MYSTERY MESSAGE

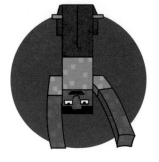

Subtract the ones, then the tens. Use the letters to fill in the blanks below and answer Alex's riddle.

1. 45
   − 21
   _____
   Y

2. 77
   − 45
   _____
   C

3. 93
   − 20
   _____
   O

4. 26
   − 12
   _____
   B

5. 32
   − 10
   _____
   U

6. 94
   − 13
   _____
   E

7. 48
   − 27
   _____
   A

8. 74
   − 23
   _____
   R

9. 68
   − 23
   _____
   M

10. 89
    − 33
    _____
    G

Q: What's the most popular ride at the *Minecraft* carnival?
Copy the letters from the answers above to find out!

___	___	___	___	___	___ -
21	45	81	51	51	24

___	___	-	___	___	___
56	73		32	22	14	81

BOSS MOB SHOWDOWN

Who has more attack power? Compare the number of times each mob has attacked a player and write in the correct symbol.

> means greater than   **<** means less than

Example   **1.** 385 **<** 391

2. 856   831

3. 445   467

4. 523   532

5. 672   668

6. 989   998

7. 723   772

Count up their wins and circle the one with the most wins below.

Wither   **Elder Guardian**

SKIP COUNT CHALLENGE

Count by 4s to help the pufferfish swim down the river and back to the ocean.

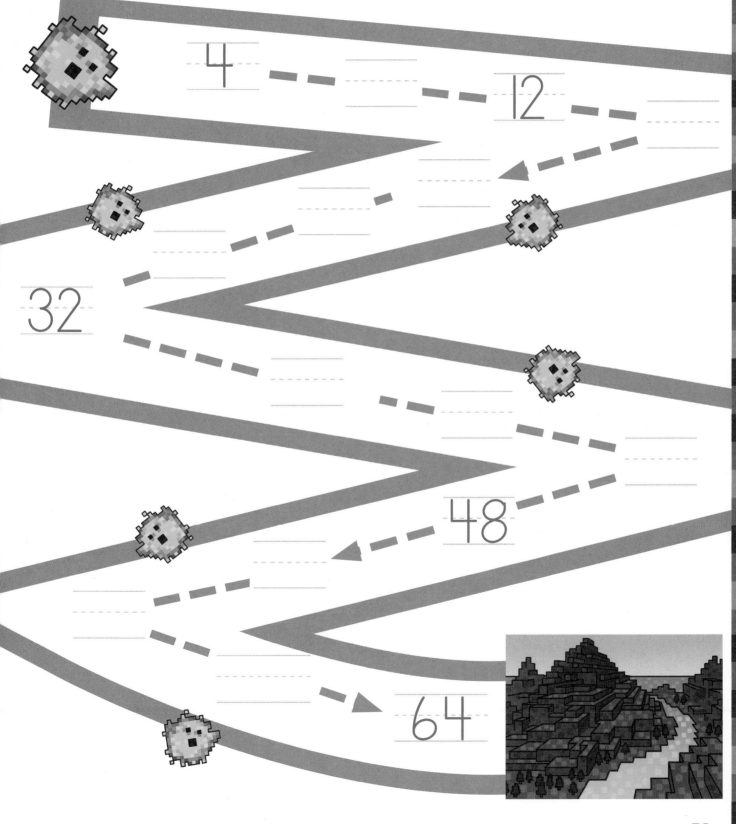

4

12

32

48

64

TELLING TIME

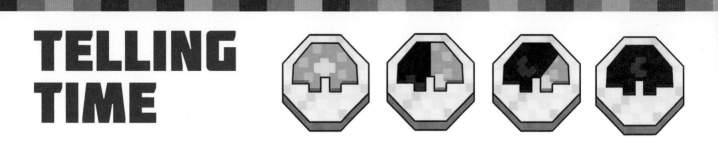

Look at the clocks below and write the time in the space provided:

Example:

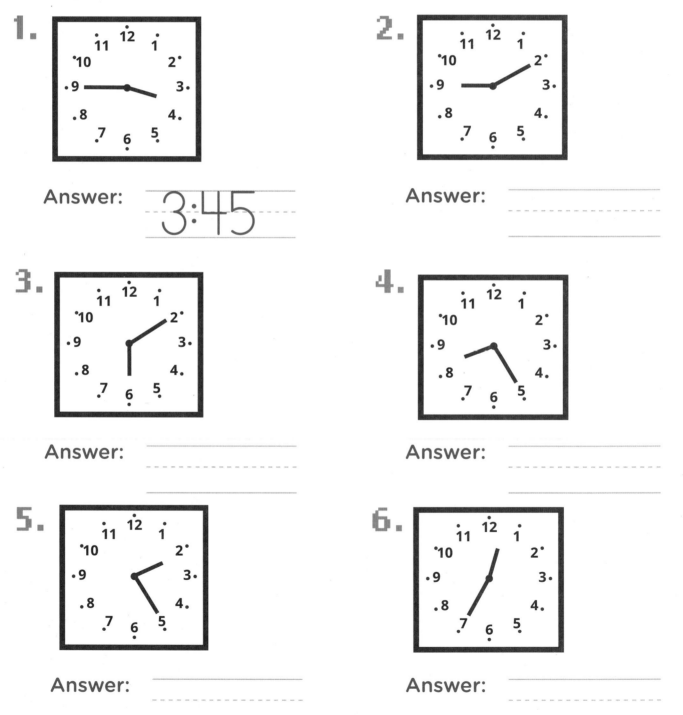

1.

Answer: 3:45

2.

Answer:

3.

Answer:

4.

Answer:

5.

Answer:

6.

Answer:

7.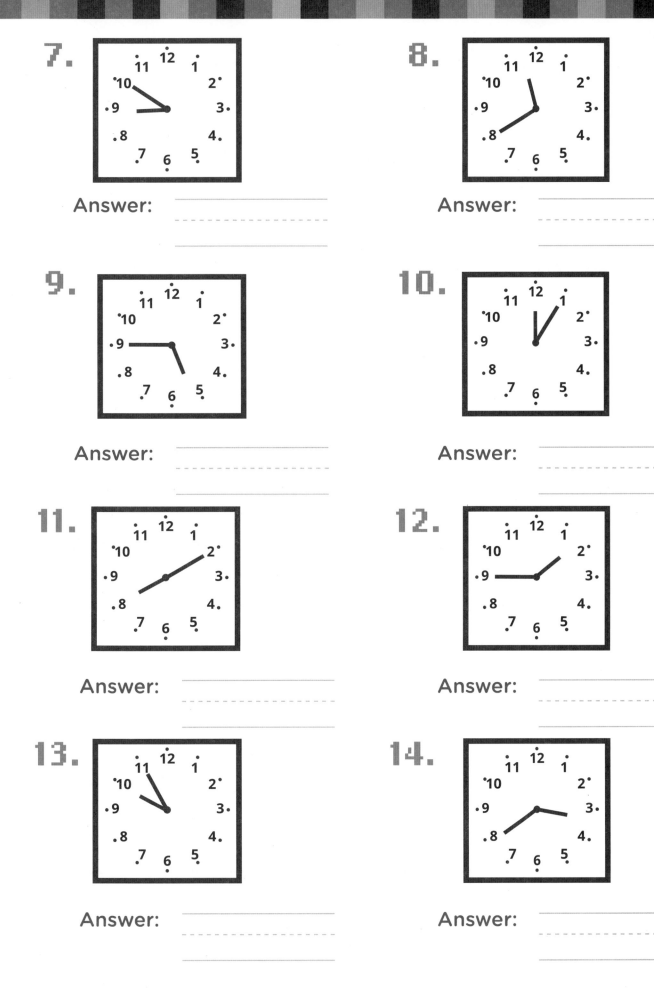

Answer: _____

8.

Answer: _____

9.

Answer: _____

10.

Answer: _____

11.

Answer: _____

12.

Answer: _____

13.

Answer: _____

14.

Answer: _____

4 SIDES ARE BETTER THAN 1

*A Minecrafter's world is full of **quadrilaterals**. Find them and circle them below.*

Hint:

Quadrilaterals are closed shapes with 4 sides.
Squares and rectangles are two kinds of quadrilaterals.

Can you find 3 quadrilaterals on this sheep?

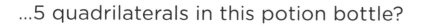

...5 quadrilaterals in this potion bottle?

...6 quadrilaterals in this tree?

Trace the quadrilaterals below:

ADDITION & SUBTRACTION MYSTERY NUMBER

There is a number hidden behind these lava blocks.
Subtract or count on to find the mystery number.

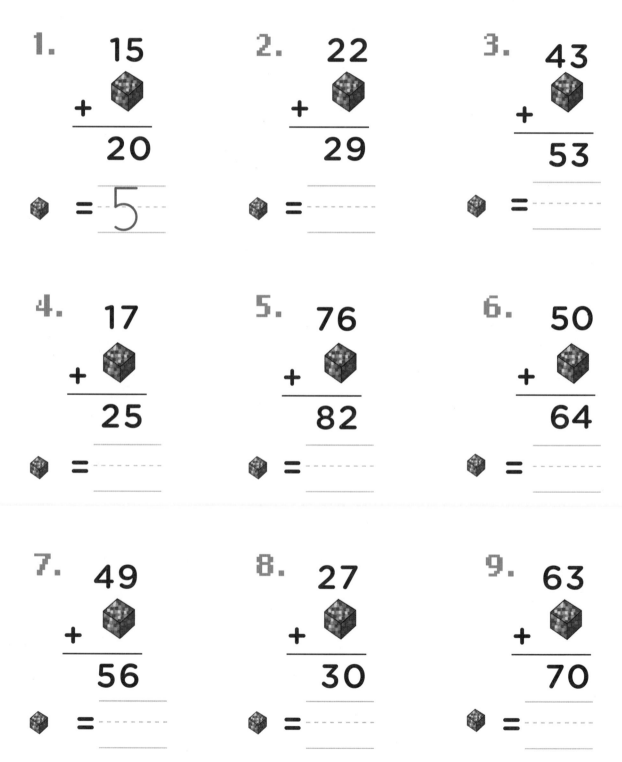

1.
```
  15
+ ▨
―――
  20
```
▨ = 5

2.
```
  22
+ ▨
―――
  29
```
▨ = _____

3.
```
  43
+ ▨
―――
  53
```
▨ = _____

4.
```
  17
+ ▨
―――
  25
```
▨ = _____

5.
```
  76
+ ▨
―――
  82
```
▨ = _____

6.
```
  50
+ ▨
―――
  64
```
▨ = _____

7.
```
  49
+ ▨
―――
  56
```
▨ = _____

8.
```
  27
+ ▨
―――
  30
```
▨ = _____

9.
```
  63
+ ▨
―――
  70
```
▨ = _____

MYSTERY MESSAGE
WITH ADDITION USING REGROUPING

Add. Use the letters to fill in the blanks below and answer the riddle.

1. $45 + 16 = $ _____ **O**
2. $36 + 7 = $ _____ **V**
3. $48 + 8 = $ _____ **C**
4. $59 + 13 = $ _____ **E**
5. $38 + 7 = $ _____ **I**

6. $25 + 9 = $ _____ **W**
7. $46 + 25 = $ _____ **R**
8. $66 + 19 = $ _____ **L**
9. $28 + 24 = $ _____ **S**
10. $47 + 16 = $ _____ **A**

Q: What happened when Steve accidentally ate a bunch of rocks?

H _ _   _ _ _ _ _
  45 52   43 61 45 56 72

_ _ _
34 63 52

G _ _ _ _ _ Y.
  71 63 43 72 85 85

SNOW GOLEM'S GUIDE TO PLACE VALUE

Identify the number that belongs in the place-value chart and write it there.

Example:

1.

Tens
3

2.

Hundreds

729

3.

Ones

829

4.

145

Hundreds

5.

632

Tens

6.

830

Ones

7.

706

Hundreds

SKIP COUNT CHALLENGE

Count by 6s to help Alex ride the runaway pig back to the pen where it belongs.

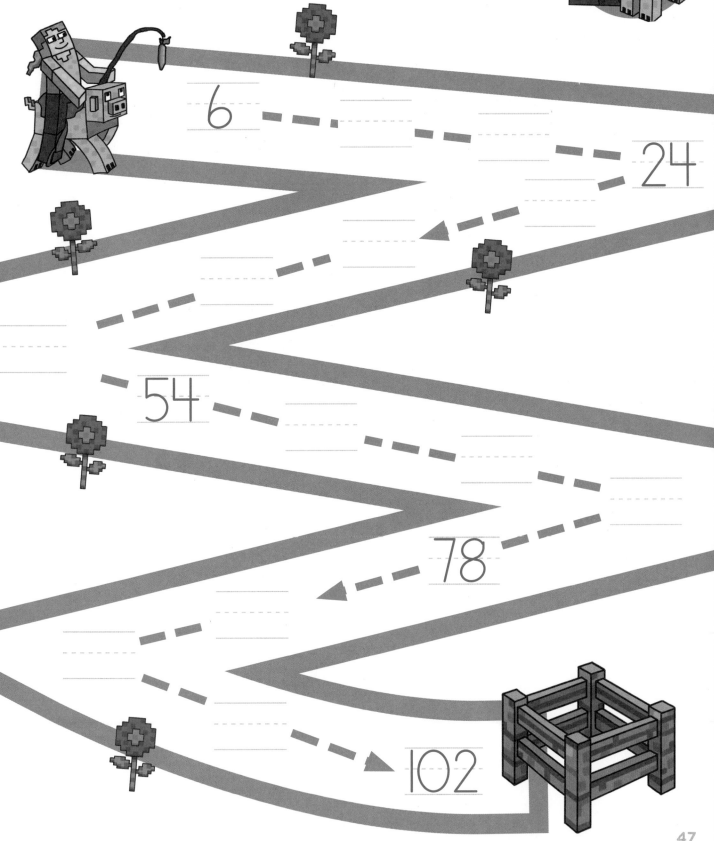

6

24

54

78

102

ANIMAL TALLY

Use the table to compare the animals that Alex and Steve have on their farms.

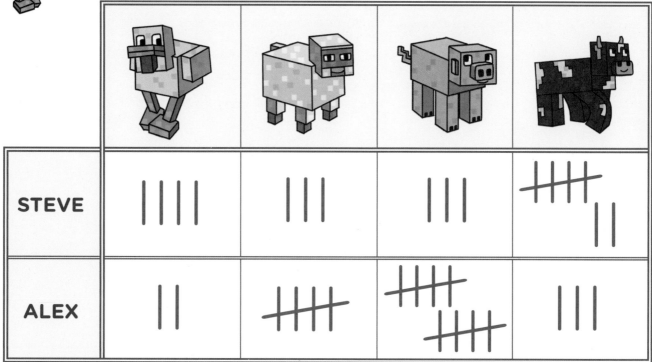

1. How many pigs does Alex keep on her farm?

2. Who has more sheep, Steve or Alex?

3. Steve and Alex both have chickens. How many *more* chickens does Steve have?

4. If Steve and Alex put their cows together on one farm, how many cows would they have?

WEAPON TALLY

Use the table to compare the weapons that Steve and Alex have crafted.

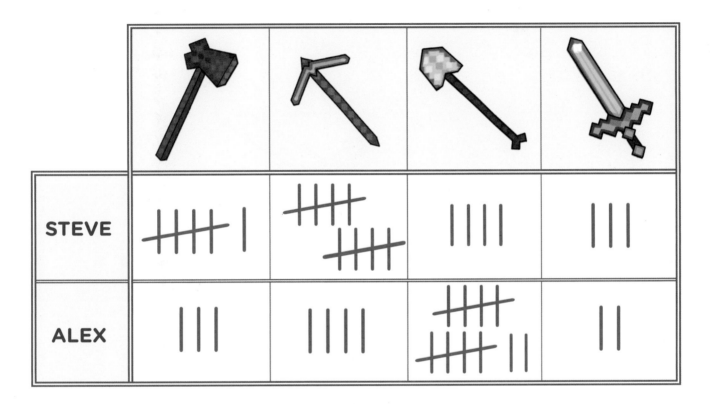

STEVE	卌 I	卌 卌	IIII	III
ALEX	III	IIII	卌 卌 II	II

1. How many diamond swords did Alex craft?

2. Steve and Alex both have pickaxes. How many *more* pickaxes does Steve have?

3. Steve and Alex both have shovels. How many *more* shovels does Alex have?

4. Who has the most axes?

ADVENTURES IN GEOMETRY: SPOT THE SHAPES

Identify and circle the shapes. Examples of each shape are provided. Color them in.

1. Can you spot: 2 **squares** in this golden sword?

2. Can you spot: 1 **trapezoid** in this diamond axe?

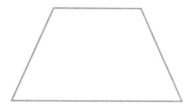

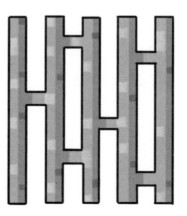

3. Can you spot 2 **rectangles** in these iron bars?

Match the name of the shape to the correct object.

1. Octagon

2. Quadrilateral

3. Oval

4. Sphere

5. Cube

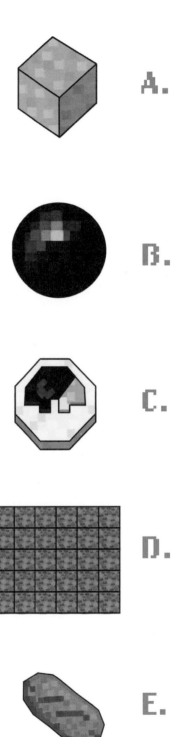

A.

B.

C.

D.

E.

WORD PROBLEMS

Write a number sentence to help you solve these word problems.

Example:

1. You break 12 dirt blocks with your diamond shovel. You also break 4 sand blocks and 6 gravel blocks. How many blocks do you break in all?

$$12 + 4 + 6 = 22$$

Answer: *22 blocks*

2. Your pumpkin pie has 12 slices. You eat 2 slices, your friend eats 3 slices, and you feed 1 slice to your pet cat. How many slices are left?

Answer: _____

3. You plant 8 flowers in your yard. A goat comes along and eats 3 of them. You plant 5 more. How many flowers do you have now?

Answer: _____

4. You grow 3 potatoes. The next day you grow 5 new potatoes. How many potatoes do you have in all?

Answer:

5. You destroy Endermen and collect 25 Eyes of Ender. You use 13 to activate the End Portal. How many Eyes of Ender do you have left?

Answer:

6. You want to make a diamond suit of armor. The helmet requires 5 diamonds, the chestplate requires 8 diamonds, and the leggings require 7 diamonds. How many diamonds do you need in all?

Answer:

7. Your house is made of 30 cobblestone blocks. An Enderman steals 12 blocks from your house. The next night, he steals 6 more blocks. How many blocks are left?

Answer:

CREEPER'S GUIDE TO PLACE VALUE

Match the number on each Creeper to the place value descriptions on the right.

Example:

1.

Tens
6

2.

Ones

3.

Tens

4.

Ones

5.

Hundreds

6.

Tens

7.

Hundreds

SKIP COUNT CHALLENGE

Count by 100s to fill in the path and help tame this
wolf with bones.

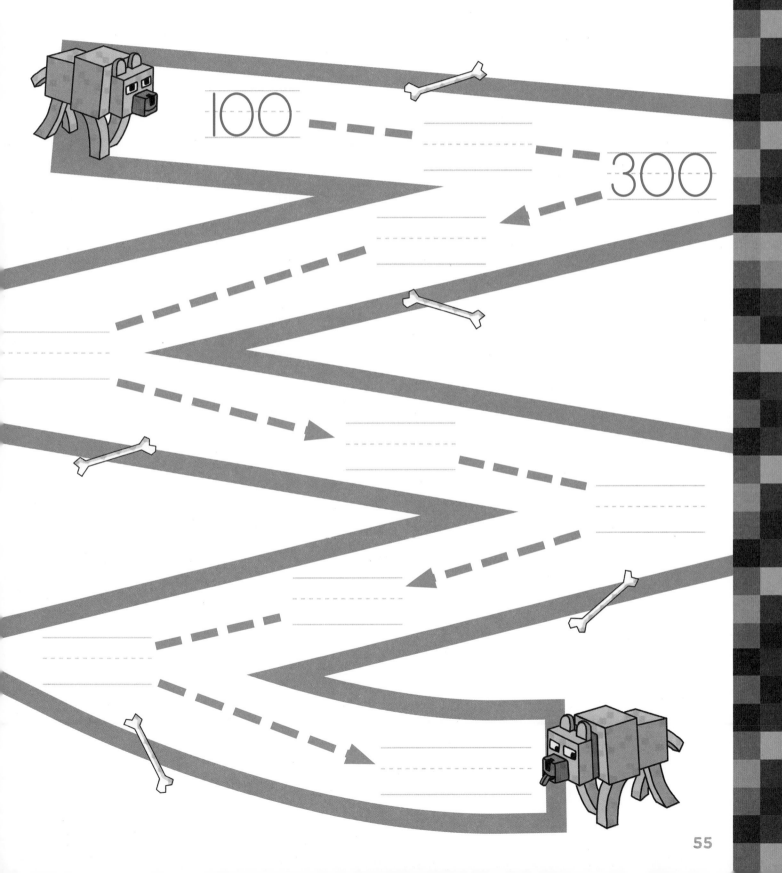

100

300

TELLING TIME

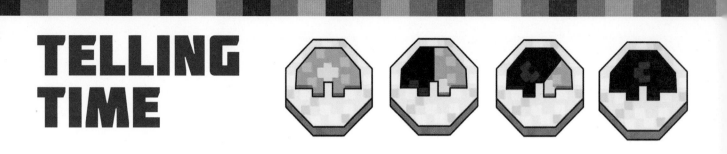

Look at the clocks below and write the time in the space provided:

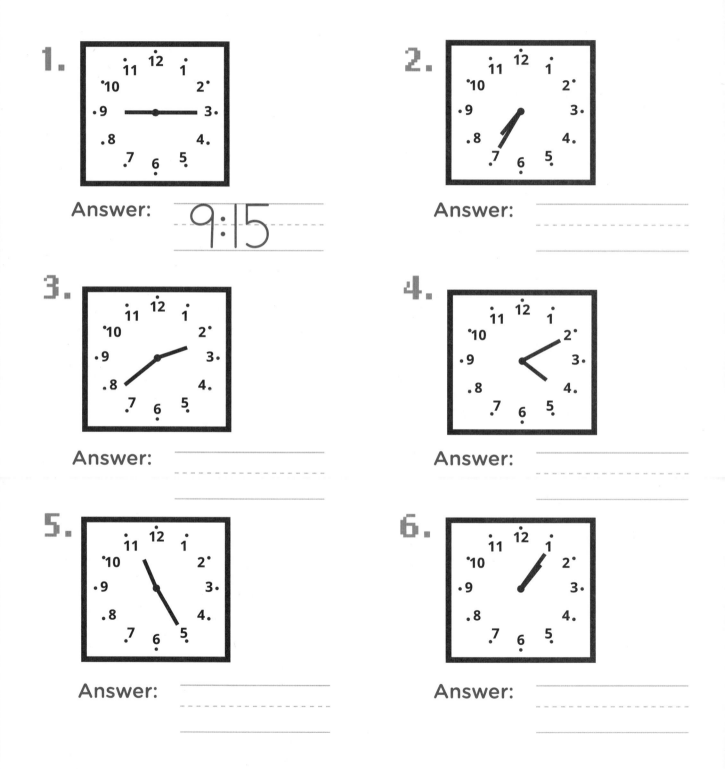

1.

Answer: 9:15

2.

Answer:

3.

Answer:

4.

Answer:

5.

Answer:

6.

Answer:

COUNTING MONEY

How much money is hidden in each treasure chest? Add up the coins to find out.

25¢ 10¢ 5¢ 1¢

1.  **32¢**

2. _____

3.  _____

4. _____

5. _____

HARDCORE MODE: Try this hardcore math challenge!
Steve looks in a treasure chest and finds 5 coins that add up
to 25¢. There is only 1 kind of coin in the treasure chest.
What coin is it?

 _____

GEOMETRY

This wooden plank is divided into 4 equal parts called fourths (or quarters). Color the wooden planks below according to the description.

1. Color: two fourths

$$\frac{2}{4}$$

2. Color: one fourth

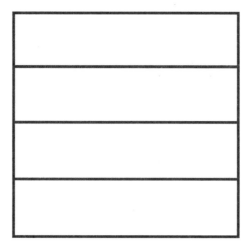

$$\frac{1}{4}$$

3. Color: four fourths

$$\frac{4}{4}$$

4. Color: three fourths

$$\frac{3}{4}$$

Match the shaded set of blocks to the correct fraction on the right.

5. 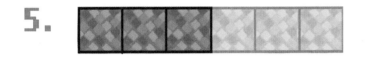 $^5/_6$

6.  $^3/_6$

7.  $^2/_6$

8.  $^4/_6$

9. 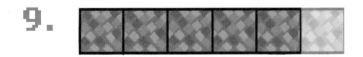 $^1/_6$

ANSWERS

Page 4: Addition by Grouping

2. 13
3. 26
4. 17
5. 15

Page 5: Mystery Message with Addition and Subtraction

2. 6
3. 14
4. 11
5. 7
6. 16
7. 5
8. 13
A: FACEBLOCK

Page 6: Zombie's Guide to Place Value

2. 3 tens 7 ones
3. 4 tens 1 ones
4. 7 tens 2 ones
5. 6 tens 3 ones
6. 5 tens 0 ones
7. 9 tens 8 ones

Page 7: Skip Count Challenge

6, 8, 10, 12, 14, 16, 20, 22, 24, 26

Page 8: Telling Time

2. 5:30
3. 10:00
4. 7:30
5. 1:30
6. 6:00

Page 9: Counting Money

2. 21 cents
3. 31 cents
4. 41 cents
5. 31 cents
6. 41 cents
7. 47 cents

Hardcore Mode:

8. 3 dimes

Page 10: Adventures in Geometry

Insert answer at the top: 4

Note: Answers may vary.

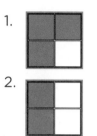

Page 11:

3. 6

4.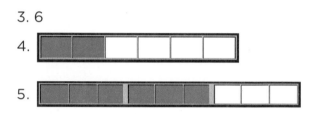

5.

6. Hardcore Mode: $\frac{1}{3}$

Page 12: Word Problems

1. 2
2. 4
3. 3

Page 13:

4. 8
5. 9
6. 3
7. 7
8. 3

Page 14: Creeper's Guide to Place Value

2. 2 tens, 7 ones
3. 8 tens, 6 ones
4. 3 tens, 2 ones
5. 7 tens, 1 ones
6. 6 tens, 0 ones
7. 5 tens, 4 ones

Page 15: Skip Count Challenge

12, 15, 18, 24, 27, 30, 36, 39

Page 16: All in a Day's Work
2. G
3. F
4. C
5. A
6. B
7. D

Page 17: Time for Clocks

Page 18: Learning About Shapes:
1. B
2. D
3. A
4. C

Page 19: Find the Shapes
5. Square
6. Circle
7. Rectangle

Note: Answers may vary.
8.

Page 20: Addition by Grouping
2. 34
3. 23
4. 20

Page 21: Mystery Message with Addition and Subtraction
2. 3
3. 16
4. 17
5. 13
6. 11
7. 9
8. 8
9. 12
10. 6

A: BLOCK PARTY

Page 22: The Ender Dragon Number Challenge
1. D
2. E
3. B
4. A
5. C

Page 23: Skip Count Challenge
15, 20, 25, 30, 40, 45, 50, 55, 60

Page 24: Comparing Rail Tracks
A. 6 ties
B. 3 ties
C. 4 ties

1. A
2. B
3. 2 ties
5. 5 ties

Page 25: Comparing Rail Tracks, cont'd

Track	Number of Ties
A	6
B	3
C	4
D	5

Page 27: Adventures in Geometry

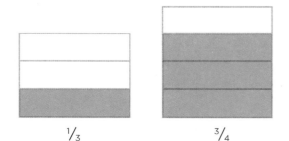

1/3   3/4

Pages 28-29: Word Problems

2. 10 hay bales
3. 4 zombies
4. 18 weapons
5. 12 cookies
6. 10 hunger points
7. 3 items
8. 12 pet cats

Page 30: Pig's Guide to Place Value

2. Hundreds:2 Tens:3 Ones:5
3. Hundreds:4 Tens:6 Ones:7
4. Hundreds:5 Tens:9 Ones:6
5. Hundreds:7 Tens:0 Ones:8
6. Hundreds:4 Tens:3 Ones:0
7. Hundreds:2 Tens:6 Ones:4

Page 31: Skip Count Challenge

112, 114, 115, 116, 117, 119, 120, 121, 122, 123

Page 32: Mobs and Monsters

	Skeleton	Ghast	Cave Spider	Snow Golem
0 Legs				X
2 Legs	X			
More than 2 Legs		X	X	

1. 2 mobs
2. 2 mobs
3. Ghast and Cave spider

Page 33: Counting Money

2. 35 cents
3. 17 cents
4. 23 cents
5. 65 cents

Hardcore Mode: 6. 83 cents

Page 34: Adventures in Geometry: Spot the Shapes

Page 36: Mushroom Addition

1. 73
2. 100
3. 74
4. 87
5. 67
6. 48
7. 75
8. 64
9. 72
10. 49
11. 81
12. 106

Hidden Message: FOREST

Page 37: Subtraction Mystery Message

1. 24
2. 32
3. 73
4. 14

5. 22
6. 81
7. 21
8. 51
9. 45
10. 56
A: A MERRY-GO-CUBE

Page 38: Boss Mob Showdown
1. <
2. >
3. <
4. <
5. >
6. <
7. <

Elder Guardian

Page 39: Skip Count Challenge
8, 16, 20, 24, 28, 36, 40, 44, 52, 56, 60

Page 40: Telling Time
2. 9:10
3. 6:10
4. 8:25
5. 2:25
6. 12:35
7. 8:50
8. 11:40
9. 5:45
10. 12:05
11. 8:10
12. 1:45
13. 9:55
14. 3:40

Page 42: 4 Sides are Better Than 1

Page 44: Addition & Subtraction Mystery Number
2. 7
3. 10
4. 8
5. 6
6. 14
7. 7
8. 3
9. 7

Page 45: Mystery Message with Addition Using Regrouping
1. 61
2. 43
3. 56
4. 72
5. 45
6. 34
7. 71
8. 85
9. 52
10. 63

A: HIS VOICE WAS GRAVELLY.

Page 46: Snow Golem's Guide to Place Value
2. 7
3. 9
4. 1
5. 3
6. 0
7. 7

Page 47: Skip Count Challenge
12, 18, 30, 36, 42, 48, 60, 66, 72, 84, 90, 96

Page 48: Animal Tally
1. 10
2. Alex
3. 2
4. 10

Page 49: Weapons Tally

1. 2
2. 6
3. 8
4. Steve

Page 50: Adventures in Geometry: Spot the Shapes

1.

2.

3.

Page 51: Adventures in Geometry: Spot the Shapes

1. C
2. D
3. E
4. B
5. A

Pages 52-53: Word Problems

2. 6 slices
3. 10 flowers
4. 8 potatoes
5. 12 Eyes of Ender
6. 20 diamonds
7. 12 cobblestone blocks

Page 54: Creeper's Guide to Place Value

2. 1
3. 3
4. 0
5. 6
6. 0
7. 8

Page 55: Skip Count

200, 400, 500, 600, 700, 800, 900, 1,000

Page 56: Telling Time

2. 7:35
3. 2:40
4. 4:10
5. 11:25
6. 1:05

Page 57: Counting Money

2. 46 cents
3. 32 cents
4. 50 cents
5. 71 cents

Hardcore Mode:

Nickel

Pages 58-59: Geometry

Note: Answers may vary.

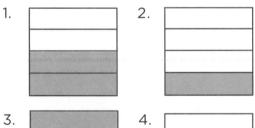

5. $\frac{3}{6}$
6. $\frac{2}{6}$
7. $\frac{1}{6}$
8. $\frac{4}{6}$
9. $\frac{5}{6}$